first snow

first snow

—tlm.

ISBN: 979-8-218-71388-1

my joy will always be yours,
and that is the truth of the first snow.

for **e**

CONTENTS

–First Snow.

I

the spell of enchantment is a curse
cast by blind greed
and ineffably the pure cause of the ultimate punishment
the eternal doom of curiosity.
–Latter Rain.

my favorite part of the day

is the night.
when the stars pop and the moon regains its glow
where all is invisible
but you are not

my favorite part of the day
is the night.
when the stars pop and the moon regains its glow
where all is invisible
~~but you are not~~
only then i am free.

where i'm from:
the coolest it ever gets is when it rains.
many of us have never seen more.
when i moved to the east,
i finally met snow.
it was gentle. it was warm.
i felt the dew melt right onto my tongue.
i thought it would be cold.

actually, the rain was colder.

it pierced through the ceilings of my house,
it lay in my skin, washed through my hair
i could never escape the rain.

with every moment wasted

i have drawn closer to
crying by your grave
screaming all the words you couldn't hear
remembering when i was more than just a given.

i am a ghost to all that i loved
you may see right through me
but you do not see me as an entity.
i never asked for reciprocation–
only hoped that before you took your last breath
perhaps you'd think of me
and wish for another.

so now i sit here
crying by your grave
wondering how many moments i lost
before losing you.

in no words may i describe
the last moments of life.

perhaps it is a beautiful thing;
i'm squeezing your hand
and you're barely grasping mine.
it is my reminder:
there is nothing to be afraid of.
this is love. isn't it lovely?

so i say to you:
let's pretend we're attending our last concert
hearing the uproar of the passerby crowd
the sirens flashing vibrant shades
of red,
and white,
and blue.

please do not judge me
for the blank stare
fallen on my face

i have been taught
to wipe my tears
before they must enter my eyes

why must i always feel like the antagonist.

i was playing by the rules!
but the fuel pummeled;
cold ashes turned to blue fire
and us–

we burned,
bibles filled with my truth
rivaled that of yours

dear prince charming
your gentle demeanor pities me
must i succumb to your cries
or shall i forever
be misunderstood?

tonight's midnight sun
shines brighter than that of a summer day

your lips glimmer in the limelight
sweet like diamonds;
saccharine in a vanishing mirror.

you are the brightest star.
without you,
our eyes could not fully comprehend
why we look–
to the moon.

hush, my darling
for with our very last kiss
you may now rest.

i dreamt of a secret garden,

just for us two.
it grows stern branches beneath the forseen
rich, deep soil
carries the seed of our love
the fruit that blossoms
most when the darkest seasons
spring to evermore

i stare at the reflection of the keys
dancing beneath your fingertips
your brown eyes shining with an eager gift
a black and white image, the sound of wood
hitting empty choruses
spurring music when you caress them

only your hands filled the scene with color
i see red, yellow, orange, and a solid blue
strung together in a delicate symphony
the melody seemed to be played in an octave higher…

11

II

to our hearts we owe
the hollow grasp of time
for in the plague of our search
we have all,
but lost our minds
–Blazing Sun.

this section may contain sensitive topics, including but not
limited to eating disorders and self harm.

there are claws who do not puncture.

eliminate our front lines, yet
never held their hearts in their hands

they who kept their pride through
and through nets of tweed
are soon to realize that threads may shrivel?
once they are cut, they cannot be still–

ties are no longer tied
as promises were never guaranteed
believe but there is nothing to believe in!
run but there is nothing to run from!
scream!
but there is nothing to scream at...
~~and so i kept my hand cupped over my mouth like a child~~
~~playing hide and seek because i knew they couldn't find out or~~
~~i'd be in trouble, or or i'd be taken; taken far far away and~~
~~never brought back home!~~
and so they sew up their wounds,
tug down their sleeves,
and go on with their lives.

if i tried to disappear

would the lipids hiding in my bones
melt into pools of sweet memories?
would the blood outside me dry out,
burn into SKINNY particles of dust?
or would i instead cement the curse

because if i am really just fat and bone, then when my grave is
purged they will see the fat sticking and clinging onto the
bone, they'll see me fat in my casket

17

i like the way my inner thighs

rub against each other
humiliating the cuts by a reminder
so long as they touch,
they will remain wounded
for as is all of my life

i feel all of them,
crawling like spiders on my skin
sticking to the insides of my brain like leeches
even the way they hurt is incomparable
to the way i made myself purge
if they heal then i can reopen them too
with just a thought i can see the tears
rushing to squeeze out in fat droplets
like my uncontrollable mouth
who eats and eats stupidly,

pumping out words like food;
that's how ANOREXIA feels
to someone like me
it consumes me
it frightens me
but i am obsessed with it

not all of us are dysmorphic
some of us look in the mirror
and see shapes we didn't
resonate with our minds
and our hearts
and our bodies?
yet others
when we feel ourselves
in the reflection
it's beautiful
and it's raw
and it's skinny
and it's motivation
it causes us drive
and discipline
and we stop
and we think about that moment
right there in the mirror
when we last looked ~~beautiful~~ skinny.
and we starve
and we starve
and we starve
and we
an

i liked playing dress up
but i never liked playing on myself

i put pretty clothes on them
and like dolls they fit like a glove
one size
but all dolls were the same size?
thin waist
well what a fucking waste
of birthday cakes
of cupcakes
of cake pops
of cake crumbs, even.
~~because when even one crumb leaves me bloated and FAT i~~
~~can't afford to even press my lips against something sweet,~~
~~and i used to CUT MYSELF OPEN because maybe i'd bleed~~
~~out the extra SUGAR in my bones…maybe i could chew~~
~~everything twice as slow so i would eat twice as less and~~
~~maybe water just tastes so fucking GOOD you know?~~

sometimes i feel like jack frost

you came to me for help
i reached out–
in a single touch,
my cold hands
already threatened your stubborn heart.

i wanted to hold you!
but my skin,
it was not home for you

i couldn't help you
even if i tried
i can't get out of this hell hole.

21

if practice makes perfect
then why am i not

rather than danced
my hands became callused
by the protruding flaws
of every wrong note

yet i see you somehow laugh
when you've made a mistake,
how could that be?

when i have spent my whole life
practicing, and practicing,
never have i ever even played once

what i have instead created
is just a monster known as repetition.

III

even the truest cannot be unconditional
as even love may be selfish, we are
(in the face of genuine terror)
–Harvest Moon.

there's a certain taste

to the autumn winds.
the air was dry,
sharp,
cold.

yet,
something about the breeze
caught between my lips–

a deafening whisper
silent shrieks of loneliness call out:
welcome,
the bitter sweetness
of the winter to come.

if i fell in love again
will i look at her
the same way i used to look at you?
will i smile
the same way i did for you?

i spent way too long on you
to give up what we had
even when it was wrong,
i still always wish it wasn't.

because even breathing was easy
if i knew you would do it with me,
even breathing was easy
when you held me through it

i wish i loved love

the way i love you
because then
i'd love the way
you love me

dead roses used to comfort my dreams

but they sprung to life when they saw you in my
nightmares–typical visions of red, velvety petals dance and
linger on the little ballerina stand in my attic;
forgotten, lonely, bursting with joy at the thought of your soft
lips. like a dull yet cutting blade at the edge of my scab.
it seems they are poking fun at me, maniacal happy eyes
staring at my bruised, bleeding breasts.

i hate the piano

but you loved it.
you leaned into each crescendo
like you leaned into our first kiss

and me, i would look at you–
listening to you.

you took me to a garden
pink daisies, ripe pomegranates.
the fruit of the gods.

the glimmering sunlight
one which betrayed my eyesight,
only illuminated your beauty.

you told your story,
and i could not.
i didn't want to, nor did i need to.

i don't play like i used to.
when i do,
i can't remember anything
except for you. your sound. your stories.

IV

when you are scared of the dark
perhaps first reconsider the truths
after all, remember
the terrors found in a shadow
are quite simply the misconception
of a light
–First Snow.

i hate to say christmas is different this year.

when really,
it is every year.

christmas does not stop someone from leaving us today.
it will not keep our families from being torn.

christmas, after all,
is just another delay
no special treatment is given for the holidays,
no god forsaken promise
that all the grief in this world
can just
disappear,

but with–or without faith in the heavens
i pray, and i pray to the <u>lord</u> unknown
that i may keep you, with me, here on the soil
of my brain.
so i cannot lose your joy or my selfish devotion
to your reminder
of a gift given to the me by the angels
which hover over the waters of our garden:
our own tenderness, severed from and by the shepherd.

in honor of my grandfather who raised me until his last day, 25 Dec 2022

i wish you knew
how the sun misses the moon

i wish you knew
how the stars adore the sunsets

i wish you knew
the way the earth stops spinning
to make way for the rain

i wish you knew
how the mist loves the earth below,
the caves yearn for just a wisp of fresh air.

how the drops of dew melt at the sight of a blue sky, the clouds
shuffle in for a closer view of the night, and the trees grasp
their leaves in hopes they could embrace forevermore!

you see?
all this does not make sense
but in what way does that make it less beautiful?

all this may be perfectly strange
but tell me,
is it not more strange
two imperfect humans–aligned as one,
are not destined to be stars?

35

you noticed i always found imperfect things
to be the most beautiful in this world
because i hated flawlessness

so maybe,
you thought i found the value in you
only by looking past the flaws

actually,
to me, you were always perfect
but even then
i liked you

if i could never have enough time

how would i see you as fruitful as you are
as i'm blinded in the sun
trapped in the blanket of night
and eternity could never be enough

through every moon, every season
i will stare at you in awe,
in mesmerizing colors
and hold you in the veins of these fields
tasting your sweetness
between each thorn

the moon meant freedom

and in each phase i saw myself
now when i look at the night
i miss my brighter star:

the gentleness of your heart,
the peace you bring with your love,
your true kindness and pure goodness,
discipline, and forbearance
—with such character
i can forget the everlasting life

my joy will always be yours,
and that is the truth of the **first snow**.

author's note

tlm stands for "the little moon", a nickname my mom gave me as a child. it's one of the only parts of childhood i carry with warmth. the moon appears often throughout this collection–it's a symbol of my yearning for freedom, independence, and parts of myself that were only starting to be revealed.

i wrote most of these poems between the ages of 15-17, when poetry was my only vulnerable outlet of expression.

fortunately, i've moved past many of the struggles cried out on these pages, but my emotions remain in words inscribed as art. they are pieces held still in a fragment of time, etched into memory by paper and pen.

croissants.
—my impression of modern art.

www.ingramcontent.com/pod-product-compliance
Lightning Source LLC
Chambersburg PA
CBHW070040070426
42449CB00012BA/3109